YOU SUCK AT COMMUNICATING

10 Formulas to Diagnose and Solve Almost Every Communication Issue

OFIR YAKOBOWICZ

Book production by MysticqueRose Publishing Services LLC

ISBN: 979-8-218-40584-7

CONTENTS

Dedication i

Foreword by Andrew Kroeze iii

Introduction v

The Fundamentals of Communication 1

Topic 1: Understanding Your Audience 5

Topic 2: Being Understood By Your Audience 11

Topic 3: Feedback 17

Topic 4: Self-Awareness 23

Topic 5: Empathy 29

Topic 6: Connection 35

Topic 7: Trust 41

Topic 8: Logical Influence 47

Topic 9: Emotional Influence 53

Topic 10: Conflict Resolution 59

Glossary 65

About the Author 69

Dedication

To my grandmother Ester and my mother Rina,
for passing on to me their wisdom and strength.

To my wife, Robin, for her unconditional support
as my wife and best friend.

To my editor, Porsché Mysticque Steele, for
helping me bring this book to life.

And to all of my family, friends, mentors, current
clients, former clients, colleagues, and everyone
else I've had the pleasure of interacting with at
some point in my life. You all have helped me
shape the content for this book - and with all your
help, we can hopefully change more lives.

Foreword by Andrew Kroeze

Imagine unlocking the full potential of everyone you communicate with; whether it's with your team, your social media followers, an in-person audience, or friends and family. This book is that key. It's not merely a guide; it's the simplest path to effective communication.

Reflecting on my journey, especially during the days leading Tribe of Buyers—a team of 20 and a coaching business that marked my life—I can't help but think, "If only I had this book back in 2021." The insights and communication formulas within these pages create the missing link I sought after to create deeper connections, drive my team forward, and engage with my audience on a level that transcends the ordinary.

I've always believed that effective communication is the power to create breakthroughs through connection—be it rallying a team around a shared vision, captivating an online audience, or delivering an unforgettable speech. The principles and strategies outlined in this book will amplify anyone's efforts.

Whether you're leading a team, crafting your next social media campaign, or standing before an eager audience, the principles laid out here are your blueprint for success. They encapsulate the very essence of engagement, turning routine interactions into extraordinary encounters.

So, if you're prepared to elevate your communication skills to inspire, lead, and connect in ways that ignite passion and drive success, then you're in for an adventure.

You're about to embark on a journey that will redefine the way you communicate, transforming not just your relationships but your entire approach to leadership and influence.

Andrew Kroeze
Founder of Masters of Fate LLC

Andrew Kroeze

Introduction

Do you ever feel like you're talking, but no one really gets what you're saying? Or maybe you end up on a totally different page than everyone else way too often? If that hits close to home, then "You Suck At Communicating" is about to be your new best friend. This isn't just a book; it's your secret weapon for crushing it in every conversation.

Why does this matter?

Here's the deal: Whether you're pitching an offer to a potential client, hashing things out with your partner, or just trying to get your point across at a family dinner, how you communicate can make or break those interactions. We live in a world where everyone's hooked on instant, quick-fire messaging, and that's where so many drop the ball with real, meaningful connections.

What's in it for you?

If you dive into these pages, you'll unlock powerful strategies that cut through the noise. You'll learn how to make your words hit home and ensure you're not just heard, but understood. I'm talking about gaining skills to build trust on the fast track, eliminate conflicts like a pro, and sway people your way, effortlessly.

Each chapter here is a goldmine of straightforward, actionable tactics. You'll fine-tune your listening, supercharge your speech, and even use your body language to your advantage. Get ready to watch your relationships transform and your persuasiveness skyrocket.

Something Important You Should Know

This book is written like an instruction manual and I intentionally left out personal stories about myself. I wanted to give you a straight shot to fixing your communication issues, and that meant removing anything I didn't think was 100% necessary. Should you be interested in learning more about me and how I've personally applied these tools, you can find me on various forms of social media.

How to Read This Book

To get the most out of this book, approach it with an open mind and a willingness to reflect on your own communication habits. Here are a few suggestions:

Take It One Chapter at a Time: Each chapter builds on the previous one, so it's best to read in order. Don't rush through; give each chapter the attention it deserves.

Reflect on Your Own Experiences: Think about your past communication successes and failures as you read. This will help you relate the concepts to your real-life situations.

Annotate and Take Notes: Highlight key points, jot down your thoughts, and note any questions that arise. This will deepen your understanding and make it easier to revisit important concepts later.

How to Implement It

Implementation is where the magic happens. Each chapter includes action items designed to help you apply what you've learned. Here's how to make the most of them:

Complete the Action Items: At the end of each chapter, there are practical exercises. Do them. These exercises are designed to reinforce the concepts and integrate them into your daily life.

Practice Consistently: Communication skills improve with practice. Make a conscious effort to apply what you've learned in your interactions, both personal and professional.

Reflect and Adjust: Regularly reflect on your progress. What's working? What isn't? Adjust your approach based on your reflections and feedback from others.

So, are you ready to step up your communication game? Let's start shaping how you connect with the world.

Trust me, by the end of this, you won't just be participating in conversations—you'll be owning them.

The Fundamentals of Communication

Context

Communication is the cornerstone for effective interaction and connection in various aspects of life, including business (directly impacting marketing, sales, fulfillment), personal relationships (partner, kids, family, friends, social surroundings), leadership (in your business, household, etc), and in conflict. This book has simple-to-remember formulas for a variety of communication scenarios. That way they're easy to use and repeatable, just like a math problem.

However, those formulas have certain fundamentals that translate between scenarios, so the point of this introduction chapter is to get you familiar with those similarities. The more we think about them in our communication, the more we can ensure that individuals can understand us, be understood by us, build trust, resolve conflicts, and even have the ability to influence others.

Why Are the Fundamentals Important?

The fundamentals of communication are important because they facilitate understanding, collaboration, and the exchange of ideas. It is the key to building strong relationships, resolving conflicts, conveying information, and achieving common goals. Without a solid grasp of communication fundamentals, individuals may struggle to express themselves, misinterpret others, and encounter challenges in both personal and professional spheres.

What Happens When Someone Gets the Fundamentals Wrong? (Failure)

When someone fails to grasp the fundamentals of communication, several negative outcomes can occur and may occur frequently, like:

- Misunderstandings: Messages are unclear or misinterpreted, leading to confusion and potential conflicts.
- Ineffective Influence: Attempts to persuade or influence others fall flat due to poor communication strategies.
- Poor Relationships: Difficulties in building trust and establishing meaningful connections with others.
- Missed Opportunities: Failing to convey important information or ideas that result in missed opportunities for growth and success.

What Happens When Someone Does It Right? (Success)

When someone applies the fundamentals of communication effectively, they experience:

- Clarity: Messages are clear, concise, and easily understood by others.

- Strong Relationships: They have the ability to build trust, rapport, and meaningful connections with diverse audiences.
- Successful Influence: Persuasion and influence efforts yield positive outcomes, and ideas are embraced by others.
- Effective Conflict Resolution: Conflicts are addressed and resolved in a constructive manner, leading to stronger relationships and better outcomes.

Keys to Success

1. Identifying Your Audience: Understanding the demographics, psychographics, and expectations of your audience is essential for tailoring your message effectively.

2. Why They Need to Hear Your Message: Demonstrating the relevance and importance of your message ensures that it resonates with your audience's needs and expectations.

3. Intentional vs. Unintentional Communication: Balancing deliberate and accidental communication while aligning verbal and nonverbal messages is crucial.

4. Verbal vs. Nonverbal Communication: Effective use of body language, gestures, posture, and vocal tonality enhances the impact of your message.

5. Internal vs. External Communication: Recognizing the significance of self-talk and internal dialogue and honing interpersonal communication skills are vital for successful communication.

Obstacles to Success

1. Lack of Awareness: Failure to recognize the importance of communication fundamentals and their impact on various aspects of life.

2. Poor Listening Skills: Inability to actively listen to and understand others, hindering effective communication.

3. Mismatched Messaging: Disconnect between verbal and nonverbal communication, leading to confusion and misinterpretation.

4. Negative Self-Talk: Internal doubts and negative self-talk can undermine external communication efforts. That is the difference between allowing your communication capability to grow or disintegrate.

5. Failure to Adapt: An unwillingness to adapt these communication fundamentals can hinder success.

Topic 1:

Understanding Your Audience

Understanding = Active Listening (Observation) + Self Clarification

Let's say you're an entrepreneur with a bunch of game-changing ideas. Unfortunately, you often find yourself misinterpreting feedback from your team.

Your biggest pain point?

You've been implementing solutions in your business that unintentionally worsen issues, leading to a negative impact on the company's mission.

However, when you combine the power of active listening with the practice of asking clarifying questions, remarkable things happen. You start receiving validation from your team, confirming that you genuinely understand what they've been telling you.

The result?

A transformation in team dynamics marked by healthier interactions and fewer misunderstandings. As a consequence, your company experiences accelerated growth, all because of the newfound clarity in communication.

Context

Understanding your audience is a fundamental aspect of effective communication. Whether you are a speaker, writer, marketer, business owner, spouse, or any other type of person trying to convey a message, it is important to have a deep comprehension of your audience's needs, preferences, and perspectives.

Why Is It Important?

Understanding your audience is important because it lays the foundation to tailor your message for them. You become more relevant, relatable, and persuasive. When you understand your audience, you can connect on a deeper level, build trust, and achieve your goals more effectively.

Equation Breakdown

1. *Active Listening (Observation)*

Active listening involves giving your full attention to the speaker and focusing on their words, tone, body language, and emotions.

> *Its Significance*
>
> When people don't actively listen, their internal bias, whether it's intentional or subconscious, can drastically skew how they continue to connect or communicate with someone.

2. *Self-Clarification*

Self-clarification involves reflecting on the information gathered through active listening and ensuring that you truly understand it.

> *Its Significance*
>
> Self-clarification helps you process and interpret the information, reducing the risk of misinterpretation or misunderstanding.

What Happens When You Do This Wrong? (Failure)

When you fail to understand your audience, several issues may arise:

- Miscommunication: Messages may be unclear or irrelevant, leading to confusion or disengagement.
- Resistance: If the audience feels misunderstood or not valued, they may resist the message or sometimes even become defensive.
- Missed Opportunities: Failure to understand your audience can result in missed opportunities to connect, persuade, or achieve your goals.

What Happens When You Do This Right? (Success)

When you successfully understand your audience:

- Your audience is more engaged and receptive to your communication because it resonates with their needs and interests.
- It's easier to build trust because the audience feels that their perspective has been acknowledged and respected.
- The chances of persuading the audience to take a desired action are significantly higher.

Keys to Success

1. Active Listening (Observation)

- Give your full attention.
- Ask open-ended questions.
- Practice empathy and nonverbal communication.
- Avoid interrupting.

2. Self-Clarification

- Reflect on what you've heard. Take some time to process before responding.
- Summarize and paraphrase to confirm your understanding. Wait to get confirmation from your audience.
- Be open to adjusting your message based on audience feedback. This is key because they'll tell you what you're getting wrong.

Obstacles to Success

- Lack of Patience: Impatience (your wants) gets in the way of active listening.
- Preconceived Notions: Prejudices and assumptions can cloud your understanding.
- Ego: An unwillingness to admit when you're unsure can get in the way of self-clarification.

Diagnosing What Part of the Equation Is Going Wrong

Confusion in Messages: If you find yourself frequently confused by feedback or responses, it might be a sign that you're not actively listening.

Resistance or Misunderstanding: Notice if your audience seems resistant or often misunderstands your points. This could indicate a need for better self-clarification.

Lack of Feedback: If your audience rarely provides feedback or seems disengaged, it might suggest you're not connecting with their needs or interests.

How to Fix This

1. Engage in a conversation with someone you know and practice active listening and self-clarification.
2. After the conversation, write down what you understood from the discussion, and compare it with what the other person intended to convey.
3. Reflect on any gaps or misunderstandings and identify areas for improvement in your understanding of the audience.

Topic 2:
Being Understood By Your Audience

Understood = Simple Idea + Clear Articulation

Let's say you're *still* a visionary entrepreneur with game-changing ideas. However, you face a challenge where your concepts often get lost in translation, leaving you frustrated.

Your pain point?

Despite having remarkable ideas, they don't resonate with others due to unclear communication. But when you embrace the power of simplifying your ideas and articulating them clearly, a transformation occurs.

Investors, team members, and stakeholders finally grasp the brilliance of your vision. The pain of being misunderstood fades and is replaced by the pleasure of investor buy-ins and the rapid acceleration of your visionary projects.

Context

Being understood by your audience is a vital aspect of effective communication. Whether you are presenting an idea, writing a report, or conveying instructions, the ability to have your message understood clearly and easily by your audience helps move things forward.

Why Is It Important?

Being understood by your audience is essential because it ensures that what you let out of your head (an idea) and what they took into theirs is the same thing. It minimizes misinterpretation, confusion, and potential errors. When you are understood, you can influence, inform, and engage your audience effectively.

Equation Breakdown

1. Simple Idea

A simple idea refers to the core message or concept you want to convey, stripped of unnecessary complexity.

> *Its Significance*
>
> A simple idea is easier for the audience to grasp and remember. It reduces the cognitive load on the audience.

2. Clear Articulation

Clear articulation involves the way you express your idea, including the choice of words, sentence structure, and delivery style.

> *Its Significance*
>
> Clear articulation ensures that your message is communicated in a straightforward and understandable manner, increasing the chances of being well-received.

What Happens When You Do This Wrong? (Failure)

When you fail to be understood by your audience, several problems may occur:

- Miscommunication: Complex or unclear ideas can lead to misinterpretation and confusion.

- Frustration: The audience may become frustrated or disengaged when struggling to comprehend the message.
- Lack of Impact: Failure to be understood diminishes the impact of your communication, making it less likely to achieve its intended purpose.

What Happens When You Do This Right? (Success)

When you ensure that you are successfully understood by your audience, you achieve:

- Clarity: The audience grasps the idea easily and quickly, reducing the risk of confusion.
- Engagement: Clear articulation keeps the audience engaged and attentive.
- Desired Outcomes: When your audience understands you, it opens up the possibility for a supportive audience, significantly increasing the likelihood of achieving your desired outcome.

Keys to Success

1. Simple Idea

- Focus on the core message.
- Eliminate jargon and unnecessary details.
- Use analogies or examples to simplify complex concepts.

2. Clear Articulation

- Choose words carefully, considering the audience's level of understanding.
- Use concise and straightforward language.

- Practice effective delivery, such as appropriate pacing and tone.

Obstacles to Success

- Overcomplication: A tendency to overcomplicate ideas can hinder the simplicity of the message.
- Lack of Clarity: Poor language choices and communication skills can impede clear articulation.

Diagnosing What Part of the Equation Is Going Wrong

Frequent Clarifications Needed: If you often have to repeat or rephrase your ideas, it could mean your core message isn't simple enough.

Confused Reactions: Observe if your audience frequently looks puzzled or asks a lot of questions. This might indicate that your articulation isn't clear.

Receiving Feedback on Clarity: Pay attention to feedback about confusion or misunderstandings. This can highlight issues with how you're presenting your ideas.

How to Fix This

1. Practice by selecting a complex idea or concept and then simplifying it as much as possible while retaining its essence.
2. Next, practice articulating this simplified idea clearly and effectively to a friend or colleague, seeking feedback on how well they understood your message.
3. Adjust your approach based on their feedback to enhance your ability to be understood by your audience.

Topic 3:
Feedback

Feedback = Active Listening (Observation) - Judgment

You're a business leader that strives for excellence but you have a difficult time taking feedback from your surroundings.

Your pain point?

Your team is afraid to open up to you and they lose motivation to take on new initiatives.

However, when you open up to active listening and remove your judgment from what you hear and observe, you start to see what issues truly need to be addressed. Your team begins to produce more feedback and your leadership becomes a catalyst for growth and innovation.

Context

Feedback is a critical component of effective communication and personal growth. It involves the process of receiving information, opinions, or evaluations about your performance, actions, or ideas. Feedback plays a vital role in professional settings, education, relationships, and self-improvement.

Why Is It Important?

Feedback is essential because it facilitates learning, improvement, and collaboration. Constructive feedback helps individuals identify strengths and weaknesses, make necessary adjustments, and achieve better results. It promotes self-awareness, fosters trust, and enhances communication.

Equation Breakdown

1. Active Listening (Observation)

Active listening in the context of feedback means paying close attention to the speaker or the information being conveyed.

> *Its Significance*
>
> Active listening ensures that feedback is based on accurate observations and not assumptions. It allows the feedback provider to gather relevant information and context.

2. Judgment

Judgment, in this equation, refers to making evaluative or critical biases while receiving feedback.

> *Its Significance*
>
> Minimizing judgment when receiving feedback helps create a safe and non-threatening environment. It encourages open dialogue and reduces the chances of defensive reactions.

What Happens When You Do This Wrong? (Failure)

When you mishandle feedback, several negative outcomes may occur:

- Miscommunication: Failing to actively listen and understand the provider's perspective can result in the provider feeling unsafe.

- Strained Relationships: Poorly received feedback can strain relationships and hinder effective collaboration by creating a lack of trust.

What Happens When You Do This Right? (Success)

When you effectively receive feedback using the equation:

- The provider is more likely to sustain open communication with you.
- You can begin to quickly understand any issues that arise.

Keys to Success

1. Active Listening (Observation)

- Give your full attention to the feedback provider.
- Ask clarifying questions to ensure you understand their perspective.
- Avoid interrupting or jumping to conclusions.

2. Minimized Judgment

- Remove any biases or preconceived thoughts from the conversation.
- Be empathetic and consider the provider's feelings and context.

Obstacles to Success

- Emotional Bias: Emotions can cloud judgment and hinder the ability to receive objective feedback.
- Lack of Empathy: Failing to consider the providers's perspective can lead to a lack of understanding and judgmental feedback.

Diagnosing What Part of the Equation Is Going Wrong

Defensive Reactions: If you find yourself feeling defensive or upset when receiving feedback, it might indicate that you're struggling to minimize judgment.

Irrelevant Feedback: If the feedback you receive feels off-base or not applicable, it could suggest that you're not fully understanding or listening to the feedback.

Lack of Feedback: If people are reluctant to provide feedback or only give surface-level comments, it might highlight a lack of openness or trust in the feedback process.

How to Fix This

1. Practice receiving feedback from a friend or colleague on a specific topic or situation.
2. Focus on actively listening to their perspective, avoiding judgment of what they say.
3. Don't interrupt them, and don't get defensive.
4. Repeat what you heard back to them to make sure you fully understood their message, and thank them for their openness.

Topic 4:

Self-Awareness

Awareness = Feedback + Self-Reflection

Picture this; you look around your social circle (professionally or personally) and you're starting to notice patterns.

Some interactions are incredibly stressful.

It feels like some individuals always try to make you feel like you're the problem. A lot of the feedback you've been getting is negative.

However, when you absorb the feedback and give yourself time for reflection, you start developing a heightened sense of self-awareness. It makes it easier to spot your triggers, patterns, and habits faster.

The result?

You're able to start building stronger bonds, solve problems quicker, and begin contributing more to develop harmony in your surroundings.

Context

Self-awareness is the conscious knowledge and understanding of your own thoughts, emotions, behaviors, strengths, weaknesses, and values. It is a crucial aspect of personal development and effective communication, as it allows individuals to better understand themselves and their impact on others. Self-awareness plays a significant role in various aspects of life, including relationships, leadership, and decision-making.

Why Is It Important?

Self-awareness is important because it forms the foundation for personal growth, effective communication, and healthy relationships. It enables individuals to make informed decisions, manage emotions, and adapt to different situations. Self-awareness also facilitates empathy and understanding of others.

Equation Breakdown

1. Feedback

Feedback involves receiving information, opinions, or evaluations from others about your behavior, performance, or actions.

> *Its Significance*
>
> Feedback provides an external perspective on your actions and behaviors, helping you see how others perceive you and your actions.

2. Self-Reflection

Self-reflection is the process of introspectively examining your thoughts, feelings, and behaviors to gain insight into your motivations, values, and beliefs.

> *Its Significance*
>
> Self-reflection allows you to connect the external feedback with your internal experiences and beliefs, leading to a deeper understanding of yourself.

What Happens When You Do This Wrong? (Failure)

When you fail to cultivate self-awareness, you may experience several negative consequences:

- Ineffective Communication: Lack of self-awareness can lead to poor communication, as you may not realize how your actions and words affect others.
- Limited Personal Growth: Without self-awareness, you may struggle to identify areas for improvement and personal growth.
- Strained Relationships: Insufficient self-awareness can lead to misunderstandings and conflicts in relationships, both personal and professional.

What Happens When You Do This Right? (Success)

When you successfully develop self-awareness using the equation, you achieve:

- Improved Communication: Self-aware individuals are better at understanding and managing their emotions and communication style.
- Personal Growth: Self-awareness fosters personal growth by identifying areas for improvement and facilitating change.
- Stronger Relationships: Self-awareness enhances empathy and understanding, leading to more positive and effective relationships.

Keys to Success

1. Feedback

- Be open to receiving feedback, even if it is critical.
- Seek feedback from diverse sources, including peers, mentors, and friends.
- Avoid becoming defensive when receiving feedback.

2. Self-Reflection

- Set aside regular time for self-reflection, such as journaling or meditation.
- Ask yourself probing questions about your thoughts, emotions, and behaviors.
- Be honest and non-judgmental when exploring your inner experiences.

Obstacles to Success

- Defensive Behavior: Reacting defensively to feedback can hinder the self-awareness process.
- Neglect: Neglecting self-reflection can impede self-awareness development.

Diagnosing What Part of the Equation Is Going Wrong

Feedback Disconnect: If you find it difficult to gain insights from feedback, it could mean you're not open enough to others' perspectives.

Internal Conflict: Notice if you struggle to align external feedback with your internal experiences. This might indicate a lack of deep self-reflection.

Repetitive Issues: If the same problems keep arising, it could suggest you're not effectively incorporating feedback into self-awareness.

How to Fix This

1. Start by seeking feedback from someone you trust on a specific aspect of your behavior or communication style.
2. Take time to reflect on the feedback you received, writing down your thoughts and emotions related to it.
3. Identify patterns or connections between the feedback and your internal experiences, considering what motivations, values, or beliefs might be influencing your behavior.
4. Use this information to make specific changes or improvements in your behavior or communication style.
5. Repeat this process periodically to continue developing your self-awareness.

Topic 5:

Empathy

Empathy = Active Listening + Emotional Understanding

You're striving to connect with your team members emotionally.

Your pain point?

A disconnected team and lackluster performance.

However, when you wholeheartedly embrace active listening and make an effort to understand your team's emotions, remarkable transformations unfold. Your team becomes more engaged, motivated, and aligned, driving extraordinary achievements and collective success.

Context

Empathy is the ability to understand and share the feelings, thoughts, and perspectives of another person. It is a crucial aspect of effective communication and building meaningful connections with others. Empathy plays a significant role in various contexts, including personal relationships, workplace interactions, and conflict resolution.

Why Is It Important?

Empathy is important because it enhances understanding and promotes positive interactions between individuals. It fosters trust, compassion, and cooperation. Empathetic individuals are better equipped to navigate conflicts, provide emotional support, and build stronger relationships.

Equation Breakdown

1. Active Listening

Active listening involves giving your full attention to the speaker, and understanding their words, tone, and body language.

> *Its Significance*
>
> As previously stated, when active listening isn't present, it will continue to hinder your ability to connect or communicate with your audience.

2. Emotional Understanding

Emotional understanding refers to the ability to recognize and comprehend the emotions, feelings, and experiences of another person.

> *Its Significance*
>
> Emotional understanding goes beyond surface-level comprehension; it involves connecting with the other person's emotions on a deeper level, which is essential for empathy.

What Happens When You Do This Wrong? (Failure)

When you fail to practice empathy effectively, several negative outcomes may occur:

- Misunderstandings: Lack of active listening and emotional understanding can lead to misunderstandings and misinterpretations.
- Disconnection: Failure to empathize can result in emotional distance and strained relationships.
- Conflict Escalation: In the heat of conflict, a lack of empathy can escalate disputes and hinder resolution.

What Happens When You Do This Right? (Success)

- When you successfully practice empathy using the equation, you achieve:
- Improved Communication: Empathetic individuals are better at conveying their understanding and support to others.
- Enhanced Relationships: Empathy fosters stronger and more positive relationships based on trust and mutual understanding.
- Conflict Resolution: Empathy plays a crucial role in resolving conflicts peacefully and effectively.

Keys to Success

1. Active Listening

- Give your full attention to the speaker.
- Avoid interrupting or rushing to judgment.
- Ask open-ended questions to encourage the other person to share their thoughts and feelings.

2. Emotional Understanding

- Put yourself in the other person's shoes.
- Pay attention to nonverbal cues, such as facial expressions and body language.
- Practice empathy without judgment or criticism.

Obstacles to Success

- Self-Centeredness: A self-centered perspective can hinder the ability to focus on the other person's emotions and experiences.
- Lack of Awareness: Insufficient awareness of your own emotions can make it challenging to understand the emotions of others.

Diagnosing What Part of the Equation Is Going Wrong

Emotional Disconnect: If you struggle to connect emotionally with others, it might indicate weak emotional understanding.

Superficial Listening: Notice if people often feel misunderstood by you. This could be a sign that your active listening needs improvement.

Receiving Feedback on Lack of Empathy: If you frequently hear that you're not empathetic, it may highlight gaps in your emotional connection skills.

How to Fix This

1. Engage in a conversation with a friend, family member, or team member about a topic they are passionate about or a personal challenge they are facing.
2. Practice active listening by giving them your full attention and avoiding interruptions.
3. Pay close attention to their emotions and nonverbal cues during the conversation.
4. After the conversation, reflect on their feelings and experiences. Try to put yourself in their shoes and imagine how they might be feeling.
5. Share your understanding and support with them, expressing empathy for their situation.
6. Continue practicing these empathetic listening skills in various conversations to strengthen your ability to empathize with others.

Topic 6:
Connection

Connection = Openness + Relatability

You're dedicated with a passion for success but sometimes it's difficult for others to approach you.

Your pain point?

A lack of connection and collaboration within your team or the people around you, leading to missed opportunities.

However, when you commit to openness and relatability, your persona starts to change. Your pain points transform into tangible benefits, including trust, camaraderie, and a shared sense of purpose among your surroundings. This newfound connection drives unparalleled success.

Context

Connection in communication refers to the establishment of a meaningful and genuine bond between individuals. It involves creating a sense of rapport, trust, and understanding that goes beyond surface-level interactions. Connection is essential in personal relationships, professional networking, and various social contexts.

Why Is It Important?

Connection is crucial because it fosters trust, cooperation, and positive interactions between individuals. It enhances the quality of relationships, leading to better collaboration, support, and a sense of belonging. In both personal and professional settings, a strong connection can lead to mutual growth and success.

Equation Breakdown

1. Openness

Openness involves being transparent, honest, and willing to share one's thoughts, feelings, and experiences with others.

Its Significance

Openness creates an environment of trust and vulnerability, encouraging others to reciprocate and share as well.

2. Relatability

Relatability refers to the ability to connect with others by finding common ground, shared experiences, or similar interests.

Its Significance

Relatability helps bridge the gap between individuals, making them feel understood and valued, which strengthens the connection.

What Happens When You Do This Wrong? (Failure)

When you fail to establish a connection effectively, several negative outcomes may occur:

- Distrust: Lack of openness can lead to suspicion and distrust in relationships.

- Disconnection: Inability to relate to others can result in a sense of isolation and disconnection.
- Missed Opportunities: Failure to connect may result in missed personal or professional opportunities.

What Happens When You Do This Right? (Success)

When you successfully establish a connection using the equation, you will achieve:

- Trust: Openness and relatability build trust, allowing for more authentic and meaningful interactions.
- Strong Relationships: Connection leads to stronger, more supportive relationships.
- Collaboration: In professional settings, strong connections can lead to productive collaboration and mutual success.

Keys to Success

1. Openness:

- Be honest and authentic in your communication.
- Share your thoughts, feelings, and experiences when appropriate.
- Listen actively and nonjudgmentally when others share with you.

2. Relatability:

- Find common interests or experiences to bond over.
- Show genuine interest in others' experiences and perspectives.
- Be empathetic and understanding of others' unique backgrounds and viewpoints.

Obstacles to Success

- Fear of Vulnerability: The fear of being judged or rejected can hinder openness.
- Lack of Interest: An unwillingness to invest time and effort in understanding others can impede relatability.

Diagnosing What Part of the Equation Is Going Wrong

Difficulty Opening Up: If you find it hard to share personal thoughts or feelings, it might suggest a fear of vulnerability.

Lack of Relatability: Notice if others don't seem to relate to you. This could mean you're not finding common ground or showing genuine interest in their experiences.

Receiving Feedback on Openness: Pay attention if people often comment on your lack of openness. This can highlight barriers to connection.

How to Fix This

1. Engage in a conversation with someone you want to connect with, whether a colleague, friend, or acquaintance.
2. Practice openness by sharing a personal experience or thought that you might not typically share.
3. During the conversation, actively listen and look for common ground or shared experiences.
4. If you discover something relatable, use it as a basis for further discussion.
5. Show empathy and understanding by asking questions and showing genuine interest in the other person's perspective.

6. Continue to practice openness and relatability in various interactions to strengthen your ability to establish connections.

Topic 7:

Trust

Trust = Experience + Consistency

Let's say you have inconsistent service delivery.

Your pain point?

Eroded client trust and wavering partnerships.

However, with consistent, reliable services, your pain points can evolve into benefits. Your clients can regain confidence, partnerships can strengthen, and your business can thrive on a foundation of trust and dependability.

This is also in personal relationships. How much you trust or don't trust someone boils down to the consistency of the experience they have.

If someone consistently drops the ball on a project, you can trust they won't get it done right. So you know to go to someone else for help.

But if someone sometimes gets their work done and other times drops the ball, you can't fully trust they are going to do it the way you want. At that point, it's on you to choose whether to extend more trust or not.

Context

Trust is the foundation of strong and lasting relationships, both in personal and professional settings. It is the belief that someone or something is reliable, honest, and capable of meeting expectations. Trust is essential for effective collaboration, open communication, and building meaningful connections.

Why Is It Important?

Trust is crucial because it creates a sense of security and confidence in relationships. It enables individuals to work together harmoniously, share sensitive information, and rely on one another. Trust is the bedrock of successful partnerships, whether in friendships, romantic relationships, or business collaborations.

Equation Breakdown

1. Experience

Experience refers to the accumulation of past interactions, observations, and knowledge about a person or entity.

> *Its Significance*
>
> Positive experiences contribute to building trust by demonstrating reliability, honesty, and competence over time.

2. Consistency

Consistency involves the repeated demonstration of trustworthy behavior, maintaining a pattern of reliability and integrity.

> *Its Significance*
>
> Consistency is essential for reinforcing trust, as it ensures that trust is not easily eroded by sporadic or unreliable actions.

What Happens When You Do This Wrong? (Failure)

When you fail to establish or maintain trust effectively, several negative outcomes may occur:

- Distrust: Lack of trust can lead to skepticism, suspicion, and wariness in relationships.
- Miscommunication: Trust issues can hinder open and honest communication, leading to misunderstandings and conflicts.
- Breakdown of Relationships: A lack of trust can ultimately result in the breakdown of relationships, both personal and professional.

What Happens When You Do This Right? (Success)

When you successfully build trust using the equation, you will achieve:

- Strong Relationships: Trust forms the basis for strong, healthy, and enduring relationships.
- Productive Collaboration: Trust facilitates effective teamwork and collaboration, leading to mutual success.
- Open Communication: Trust enables open and transparent communication, fostering understanding and problem-solving.

Keys to Success

1. Experience

- Demonstrate reliability and honesty in your actions and interactions.

- Seek opportunities to build positive experiences and establish a track record of trustworthiness.

2. Consistency

- Maintain a consistent pattern of behavior that aligns with your values and principles.
- Avoid making promises or commitments that you cannot fulfill.
- Address any inconsistencies promptly and transparently to rebuild trust if it's been compromised.

Obstacles to Success

- Betrayal of Trust: A breach of trust can be a significant obstacle to rebuilding it, requiring time and effort.
- Miscommunication: Poor communication can lead to misunderstandings that erode trust.

Diagnosing What Part of the Equation Is Going Wrong

History of Untrustworthiness: Reflect on past interactions where trust was broken. This can indicate where you need to rebuild reliability.

Inconsistent Behavior: Notice if there's a gap between what you say and what you do. This inconsistency can erode trust.

Frequent Doubts from Others: If people often express doubts about your reliability, it might suggest that your consistency needs improvement.

How to Fix This

1. Identify a relationship or situation where trust may be lacking or needs improvement, whether it's a personal relationship or professional partnership.
2. Reflect on your past interactions and experiences in that relationship.
3. Consider where trust may have been compromised or where consistency may have faltered.
4. Take proactive steps to rebuild trust, such as making and fulfilling commitments, communicating openly and honestly, and demonstrating reliability over time.
5. Continue to nurture and reinforce trust by consistently delivering on your promises and maintaining open communication.

Topic 8:
Logical Influence

Logical Influence = Idea + New Information

Imagine that you're trying to persuade board members, team members, and many others, about strategic decisions you want to make.

Your pain point?

They don't fully grasp why your ideas make sense, leading to missed opportunities.

However, with a clear idea and compelling information, your pain transforms into benefits—you get support, decisive actions, and organizational growth that aligns with your vision.

Context

Logical influence refers to the ability to persuade or convince others through rational and reasoned arguments. It involves presenting ideas and supporting them with new, relevant information or evidence. Logical influence plays a crucial role in decision-making, problem-solving, and effective communication in various domains, including business, politics, academia, and sometimes personal relationships.

Why Is It Important?

Logical influence is important because it allows individuals to present their ideas and proposals effectively, increasing the likelihood of gaining support, agreement, or buy-ins from others. It is a valuable skill for leaders, negotiators, educators, and anyone seeking to make a compelling case or influence outcomes.

Equation Breakdown

1. Idea

An idea is a concept, proposal, or argument that forms the basis of the message.

Its Significance

A clear and compelling idea serves as the foundation for logical influence, providing a direction for communication.

---

2. New Information

New information consists of facts, data, evidence, or insights that support and enhance the idea being presented newly to the audience.

Its Significance

New information adds credibility and persuasiveness to the argument, making it more compelling and convincing.

What Happens When You Do This Wrong? (Failure)

When you fail to use logical influence effectively, several negative outcomes may occur:

- Lack of Conviction: Without a clear idea or compelling new information, the argument may lack conviction and fail to persuade.

- Misunderstanding: Poorly articulated ideas or irrelevant information can lead to confusion and misunderstanding.
- Resistance: If the argument lacks logical coherence or sound evidence, it may face resistance or rejection.

What Happens When You Do This Right? (Success)

When you successfully use logical influence using the equation, you will achieve:

- Persuasion: A well-structured argument with a clear idea and relevant new information is more likely to persuade others.
- Informed Decisions: Logical influence supports informed decision-making by providing credible and compelling reasoning.
- Problem-Solving: Effective use of logical influence can lead to a supportive audience when solving their problems.

Keys to Success

1. Idea

- Clearly define your idea or argument.
- Ensure that the idea is relevant to the context and aligns with the audience's interests and values.
- Craft a persuasive and concise statement of the idea.

2. New Information

- Gather relevant data, facts, or evidence to support your idea.

- Ensure the information is accurate, up-to-date, and credible.
- Present the information in a clear and organized manner.

Obstacles to Success

- Lack of Preparation: Inadequate research or preparation can result in a weak argument.
- Emotional Bias: Allowing emotions to override logic can hinder the effectiveness of logical influence.

Diagnosing What Part of the Equation Is Going Wrong

Unclear Message: If your audience often seems confused, it might mean your idea isn't clearly defined.

Lack of Persuasion: Notice if your arguments fail to persuade. This could indicate that your supporting information isn't strong or relevant enough.

Receiving Feedback on Logic: Pay attention if people often find your reasoning unconvincing. This can highlight gaps in the logic or information you're presenting.

How to Fix This

1. Select a topic or issue where you want to persuade or influence someone's opinion or decision.
2. Clearly define your idea or argument related to the chosen topic.
3. Research and gather new, relevant information or evidence that supports your idea.

4. Organize your thoughts and information into a persuasive presentation or argument.

5. Practice presenting your logical influence to a friend, colleague, or mentor, seeking feedback on the clarity, persuasiveness, and relevance of your idea and the strength of the new information.

6. Refine your argument based on feedback and continue to practice using logical influence in various contexts to improve your persuasive skills.

Topic 9:
Emotional Influence

Emotional Influence = Idea + Emotional Connection

You want to motivate your team to embrace a challenging project.

Your pain point?

A disengaged team that lacks enthusiasm for the mission.

However, when you combine your clear idea with emotionally influential messages, you trigger a remarkable shift. Your pain points evolve into benefits, including inspired teams, enthusiastic project involvement, and success stories that resonate deeply with your team.

Context

Emotional influence refers to the ability to persuade or motivate others by appealing to their emotions and creating a strong emotional connection. It involves presenting ideas or messages that resonate emotionally with the audience. Emotional influence is essential in various contexts, including marketing, leadership, public speaking, and personal relationships.

Why Is It Important?

Emotional influence is important because it can inspire action, build trust, and create lasting connections. Emotions play a significant role in decision-making and behavior, and individuals who tap into these emotions can effectively inspire others to be in action or have powerful mindset shifts.

Equation Breakdown

1. Idea

An idea serves as the core message or argument that you want to convey emotionally.

> *Its Significance*
>
> A clear and compelling idea provides direction and substance to emotional influence, ensuring that the emotional connection serves a purpose.

2. Emotional Connection

Emotional connection involves evoking and relating to the emotions, feelings, and experiences of the audience.

> *Its Significance*
>
> Emotional connection helps the audience connect on a deeper level with the idea, making it more memorable and persuasive.

What Happens When You Do This Wrong? (Failure)

When you fail to use emotional influence effectively, several negative outcomes may occur:

- Lack of Engagement: Without an emotional connection, the audience may remain disengaged or indifferent to the message.

- Misalignment: A misalignment between the emotional appeal and the idea can result in confusion or distrust.
- Resistance: Attempting to manipulate emotions insincerely can lead to resistance or skepticism.

What Happens When You Do This Right? (Success)

When you successfully use emotional influence using the equation, you will achieve:

- Motivation: An emotionally resonant message can motivate the audience to take action or adopt a particular perspective.
- Connection: Emotional influence fosters a strong connection between the communicator and the audience, building trust and rapport.
- Memorability: Messages that evoke emotions are more memorable and impactful.

Keys to Success

1. Idea

- Clearly define your idea or argument, ensuring it aligns with the emotional appeal you intend to use.
- Craft a persuasive and emotionally resonant statement of the idea.
- Ensure that the idea is relevant and meaningful to the audience.

2. Emotional Connection

- Identify the emotions you want to evoke in the audience.

- Use storytelling, anecdotes, or relatable examples to create an emotional connection.
- Show genuine empathy and understanding of the audience's emotions and experiences.

Obstacles to Success

- Inauthenticity: Attempts to manipulate emotions insincerely can be detected and lead to distrust.
- Overemphasis on Emotion: Overly emotional appeals without a clear idea can be seen as manipulative or lacking substance.

Diagnosing What Part of the Equation Is Going Wrong

Emotional Disconnect: If your audience doesn't seem emotionally engaged, it might suggest that your connection isn't strong enough.

Inauthentic Reactions: Notice if people perceive your emotional appeals as insincere. This can indicate a lack of genuine emotional connection.

Receiving Feedback on Emotional Impact: If your messages don't resonate emotionally, it may highlight a need to better align your emotional appeals with your core idea.

How to Fix This

1. Choose a message or idea that you want to convey emotionally to a specific audience.
2. Define your idea clearly and concisely.
3. Identify the emotions you want to evoke in the audience based on your message.

4. Craft a narrative or message that incorporates the emotional appeal and aligns with your idea.

5. Practice delivering your emotionally influential message to a friend, family member, or colleague, and ask for their feedback on the emotional impact and alignment with the idea.

6. Continue refining and practicing your emotional influence skills in various contexts to improve your ability to connect with others on an emotional level.

Topic 10:
Conflict Resolution

Conflict Resolution = (Me + Others) - Issue

You're a driven entrepreneur surrounded by interpersonal conflicts.

Your pain point?

A team that's often at odds, leading to stagnation and missed opportunities.

However, with facilitated discussions and conflict resolution strategies, you turn your pain into benefits. The benefits include a united team, a renewed sense of purpose, and a thriving business poised for greatness.

Context

Conflict resolution is the process of addressing and resolving disputes, disagreements, or conflicts between parties. It involves finding mutually agreeable solutions to issues or conflicts that may arise in various settings, including personal relationships, workplaces, and communities. Effective conflict resolution promotes understanding, cooperation, and the restoration of positive relationships.

Why Is It Important?

Conflict resolution is essential because it helps prevent misunderstandings from escalating into more significant issues, reduces tension, and fosters collaboration. It enables parties to address their concerns, find common ground, and work towards mutually beneficial outcomes. Effective conflict resolution is crucial for maintaining healthy relationships[1] and productive environments.

Equation Breakdown

1. (Me + Others)

Me + Others represents your team. Ideally, you all want the same thing and there's an issue getting in the way.

> *Its Significance*
>
> Understanding the perspectives and needs of all parties is essential for finding solutions that are acceptable to everyone involved.

2. Issue

The issue represents the specific problem, disagreement, or conflict that needs to be resolved.

> *Its Significance*
>
> Identifying and defining the issue accurately is crucial for addressing the root cause of the conflict and finding effective solutions.

What Happens When You Do This Wrong? (Failure)

When conflict resolution is not handled effectively, several negative outcomes may occur:

---

1. The big key takeaway from the formula is to separate the people from the problem! It's you and the people versus the problem. You are all on the same team.

- Escalation: Unresolved conflicts can escalate, leading to further tension and damage to relationships.
- Misunderstanding: Failing to understand and address the underlying issues can result in persistent conflicts.
- Disengagement: Parties may disengage or avoid each other, hindering collaboration and productivity.

What Happens When You Do This Right? (Success)

When you successfully resolve conflicts using the equation, you will achieve:

- Improved Relationships: Effective conflict resolution leads to the restoration of positive relationships and enhanced trust.
- Cooperation: Parties are more likely to work together harmoniously after conflicts are resolved.
- Problem Resolution: Addressing the underlying issues allows for the resolution of specific problems and prevents future conflicts.

Keys to Success

1. Parties

- Actively listen to the perspectives and concerns of all parties involved.
- Show empathy and understanding for the emotions and needs of each party.
- Encourage open and respectful communication between parties.

2. Issue

- Define the issue clearly and objectively, focusing on the underlying problem rather than personal attacks.
- Collaboratively identify the root causes of the conflict and potential solutions.
- Work together to reach a mutually agreeable resolution that addresses the issue.
- Remember that the people and the issue should be separate.

Obstacles to Success

- Emotional Reactions: Strong emotions can impede rational problem-solving during conflicts.
- Lack of Communication: Ineffective or hostile communication can hinder the resolution process.

Diagnosing What Part of the Equation Is Going Wrong

Escalating Conflicts: If conflicts often escalate instead of resolving, it could indicate that parties aren't listening to each other effectively.

Persistent Issues: Notice if the same conflicts keep arising. This might mean the underlying issue isn't being addressed properly.

Disengagement: If parties withdraw from conflict discussions, it may suggest a lack of empathy or understanding in the resolution process.

How to Fix This

1. Identify a recent conflict or disagreement that you have observed or been involved in.
2. List the parties or individuals involved and their respective perspectives or concerns.
3. Clearly define the underlying issue that led to the conflict.
4. Practice active listening and empathy by engaging in a conversation with the parties involved, encouraging them to share their perspectives and emotions.
5. Collaboratively work with the parties to identify potential solutions and reach a resolution that addresses the issue and satisfies the needs of all parties.
6. Reflect on the experience and the effectiveness of the conflict resolution process and continue to apply these skills in future efforts.

Glossary

Active Listening
The practice of fully engaging and focusing on what others are saying, both verbally and nonverbally, to understand their perspectives and feelings.

Clear Articulation
The skill of expressing ideas or messages in a manner that is easily understood by others, using clear and concise language.

Conflict Resolution
The process of addressing and resolving disputes or conflicts between parties to reach a mutually agreeable solution, focusing on understanding the perspectives of all involved and identifying the root cause of the issue.

Consistency
The quality of being dependable and uniform in actions or outcomes over time, which builds trust and reliability. It involves maintaining a consistent pattern of trustworthy behavior.

Connection
The establishment of a strong and meaningful relationship or bond with others, often based on shared experiences or values. It requires openness and relatability.

Emotional Connection

The establishment of a deep and resonant emotional bond or attachment with others, fostering empathy and understanding. It goes beyond surface-level interactions to create meaningful connections.

Emotional Influence

The capacity to persuade or motivate others by appealing to their emotions and forming a strong emotional connection. It involves presenting ideas that resonate emotionally with the audience.

Emotional Understanding

The capacity to comprehend and relate to the emotions and experiences of others, demonstrating empathy. It involves recognizing and interpreting emotional cues.

Empathy

The ability to understand and share the feelings and perspectives of others, demonstrating emotional intelligence and compassion. It is key to building strong, trusting relationships.

Experience

The accumulated knowledge and expertise gained through practical involvement and exposure to various situations or tasks. Positive experiences contribute to building trust.

Feedback

Information, opinions, or reactions provided by others, often aimed at improving understanding or performance. Effective feedback involves active listening and minimizing judgment.

Idea
A thought, concept, or proposition that forms the basis of a message or argument, often representing a unique perspective or solution. It should be clear and compelling.

Logical Influence
The ability to persuade or convince others through the presentation of clear ideas and relevant new information, supported by rational reasoning.

New Information
Fresh or novel data, facts, or insights that add value to an idea or argument, often used to support logical influence. It makes the argument more compelling and credible.

Openness
A willingness to be transparent, honest, and receptive in interactions, creating an environment of trust and communication. It encourages others to reciprocate openness.

Self-Awareness
A deep understanding of one's own thoughts, emotions, behaviors, and their impact on oneself and others. It is crucial for personal growth and effective communication.

Self-Clarification
The process of seeking clarification and understanding within oneself to ensure accurate communication and self-awareness. It reduces the risk of misinterpretation.

Self-Reflection
The process of introspection and thoughtful examination of one's thoughts, actions, and experiences, often leading to personal growth. It connects external feedback with internal experiences.

Simple Idea
A clear and straightforward concept or message that is easy for others to grasp, often representing the essence of a complex idea. Simplifying ideas makes them more understandable and memorable.

Trust
The belief and confidence in the reliability, integrity, and consistency of a person, organization, or system, often built through experience and consistent behavior. Trust is fundamental to strong relationships.

About the Author

Ofir Yakobowicz is renowned for his profound ability to connect and communicate with almost anyone around him. He's a gifted listener who excels in empathetically guiding those around him through personal and professional challenges, expressing transformative insights, and emphasizing that life improvement begins with enhanced communication. His skill in simplifying complex concepts has aided in conflict resolution, strengthening interpersonal relationships, and has also made emotional processing and spiritual releasing much more obtainable. Friends and clients often describe conversations with Ofir as enlightening, leaving them feeling understood, empowered, and equipped with new perspectives.

Connect with Ofir